967
.62
Klla

AGIKUYU

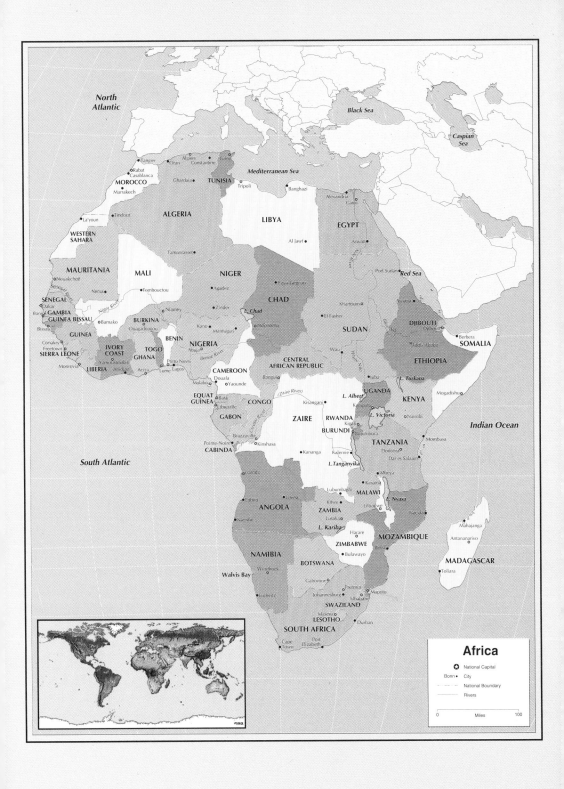

North
Atlantic

Black Sea

Caspian
Sea

Tangier
Algiers Constantine
Rabat Oran Tunis
Casablanca
MOROCCO Ghardaia
TUNISIA
Tripoli
Marrakech
Mediterranean Sea
Banghazi
Alexandria
La'youn Tindouf
Cairo
ALGERIA
LIBYA
EGYPT
WESTERN
SAHARA Al Jawf
Aswan
Tamanrasset
Port Sudan Red Sea
MAURITANIA MALI NIGER
Nouakchott
Agadez Faya-Largeau
Nema Tembouctou CHAD
Zinder Khartoum
SENEGAL Niamey L. Chad DJIBOUTI
Dakar Niger River Kano El Fasher Adis Abeba Berbera
Banjul GAMBIA Bamako Maiduguri Ndjamena
GUINEA BISSAU BURKINA SUDAN ETHIOPIA SOMALIA
Bissau Ouagadougou Wau
GUINEA BENIN NIGERIA Mogadishu
Conakry Freetown TOGO Abuja Benue River CENTRAL L. Turkana
SIERRA LEONE IVORY GHANA AFRICAN REPUBLIC
Monrovia COAST Lome Lagos CAMEROON Bangui UGANDA KENYA
LIBERIA Yamoussoukro Accra Douala L. Albert
Abidjan Porto Novo Yaounde Kampala Nairobi
EQUAT Malabo Kisangani L. Victoria Mombasa
GUINEA Bata CONGO Zaire River RWANDA
GABON Libreville ZAIRE Kigali Indian Ocean
Brazzaville BURUNDI
Pointe-Noire Bujumbura TANZANIA
CABINDA Kinshasa Dodoma
South Atlantic Kananga Kalemie Dar es Salaam
L.Tanganyika
Luanda Kasama
Lubumbashi MALAWI
Luena Kitwe L. Nyasa
Cabinda ANGOLA ZAMBIA Lilongwe Nacala
Namibe Lusaka
L. Kariba Harare MOZAMBIQUE Mahajanga
ZIMBABWE Beira Antananarivo
NAMIBIA Bulawayo
BOTSWANA MADAGASCAR
Walvis Bay Windhoek Toliara
Gaborone
Luderitz Pretoria
Johannesburg Maputo
Mbabane
SWAZILAND
Maseru
LESOTHO Durban
SOUTH AFRICA
Cape Port
Town Elizabeth

Africa

⊛ National Capital

Bonn • City

– · – National Boundary

—— Rivers

0   Miles   100

The Heritage Library of African Peoples

AGIKUYU

Wanjiku Mukabi Kabira, Ph.D.

THE ROSEN PUBLISHING GROUP, INC.
NEW YORK

Published in 1995 by The Rosen Publishing Group, Inc.
29 East 21st Street, New York, NY 10010

SEP 1 3 2005

Copyright 1995 by The Rosen Publishing Group, Inc.

First Edition

Manufactured in the United States of America

Library of Congress Cataloging-in-Publication Data

Kabira, Wanjiku Mukabi.
   Agikuyu / Wanjiku Mukabi Kabira. — 1st ed.
     p. cm. — (The Heritage library of African peoples)
   Includes bibliographical references and index.
   ISBN 0-8239-1762-2
   1. Kikuyu (African people)—History—Juvenile literature.
2. Kikuyu (African people)—Social life and customs—Juvenile
literature. [1. Kikuyu (African people)] I. Title. II. Series.
DT433.545.K55K32   1995
306'.089'96395406762—dc20   94-26118
                                                 CIP
                                                 AC

Contents

INTRODUCTION

THERE IS EVERY REASON FOR US TO KNOW
something about Africa and to understand its
past and the way of life of its peoples. Africa is a
rich continent that has for centuries provided
the world with art, culture, labor, wealth, and
natural resources. It has vast mineral deposits,
fossil fuels, and commercial crops.

But perhaps most important is the fact that
fossil evidence indicates that human beings
originated in Africa. The earliest traces of
human beings and their tools are almost two
million years old. Their descendants have
migrated throughout the world. To be human is
to be of African descent.

The experiences of the peoples who stayed in
Africa are as rich and as diverse as of those who
established themselves elsewhere. This series of
books describes their environment, relationships,
and their customs and beliefs. The books present
the variety of languages, histories, cultures, and
religions that are to be found on the African
continent. They demonstrate the historical link-
ages between African peoples and the way contemporary Africa has been affected by European
colonial rule.

Africa is large, complex, and diverse. It
encompasses an area of more than 11,700,000

square miles. The United States, Europe, and India could fit easily into it. The sheer size is an indication of the continent's great variety in geography, terrain, climate, flora, fauna, peoples, languages, and cultures.

Much of contemporary Africa has been shaped by European colonial rule, industrialization, urbanization, and the demands of a world economic system. For more than seventy years, large regions of Africa were ruled by Great Britain, France, Belgium, Portugal, and Spain. African peoples from various ethnic, linguistic, and cultural backgrounds were brought together to form colonial states.

For decades Africans struggled to gain their independence. It was not until after World War II that the colonial territories became independent African states. Today, almost all of Africa is ruled by Africans. Large numbers of Africans live in modern cities. Rural Africa is also being transformed, and yet its people still engage in many of their age-old customs and beliefs.

Contemporary circumstances and natural events have not always been kind to ordinary Africans. Today, however, new social movements and technological innovations pose great promise for future development.

George C. Bond
Institute of African Studies
Columbia University, New York City

According to the Agĩkũyũ, their origins are found at the top of Mt. Kenya.

1

THE LAND OF THE AGIKUYU

THE AGIKUYU SAY THAT A LONG, LONG TIME ago, Ngai created a man and a woman named Gikuyu and Mumbi. They had children, who were the first Agikuyu. Nagi took Gikuyu to the highest peak of his mountain home, Kirinyaga (Mt. Kenya), and showed him the beauty of the land below him. It was a land flowing with milk and honey, a land of ridges, hills, rivers, forests, and grassy areas. Gikuyu admired the land, and Ngai said to him, "Behold your land. This is for you and for your generations to come." Gikuyu and Mumbi then walked down the slopes of Mt. Kenya with joy in their hearts.

The majority of the Agikuyu, or Gikuyu people, are concentrated in five districts of Kenya: Kiambu, Nyeri, Murang'a, Kirinyaga, and Nyandarua. Most people live in Central Province. Other live in

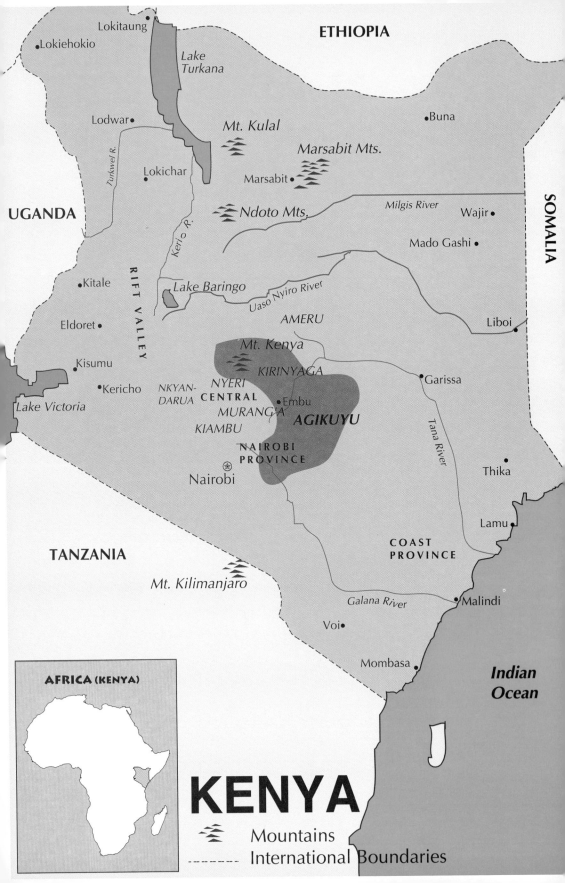

the Rift Valley Province, in Nairobi Province, Coast Province, and many other parts of Kenya. The majority of the people in Nairobi are of Gikuyu origin.

The Central District lies on the southern and eastern slopes of Mt. Kenya. Here are many semipermanent rivers such as the Thagana and Chania, and many streams. The province rarely suffers drought. There are long rains in April and May, and shorter rains occur in July–August and November.

Mt. Kenya is 17,000 feet above sea level, the second-highest mountain in Africa after Kilimanjaro. Central Province also borders the great Rift Valley. It has good communication and transportation systems, with tarmac and all-weather roads in most parts of the province.

Almost 100 percent of the Agikuyu people speak the Gikuyu language. Most people under 50 also know Kiswahili and English, languages important for people who live in a multicultural city and engage in business with other groups and countries.

The Agikuyu are also called Akikuyu and Kikuyu. A Gikuyu is one member of the Agikuyu people.

▼ ECONOMY ▼

The Agikuyu are the largest single community in Kenya, numbering about six million in a country of about 25 million.

Two styles of granaries used to store harvested grains.

Like many other communities, the Agikuyu began as hunters and gatherers. A group of Agikuyu were still practicing these activities as late as the mid-19th century. They used spears, arrows, and clubs to hunt bushbucks, buffalo, rhinoceros, wild pigs, and warthogs. Today Central Province is much different, with a dense population and heavy agriculture.

Traditional foods such as millet, cow peas, bananas, sweet potatoes, yams, arrowroot, sugarcane, and cassava are still grown. With the coming of colonialism, maize, beans, potatoes, coffee, and tea were introduced. In the past fifty years greater emphasis has been placed on cash crops than on food crops. The main cash crops have been coffee, tea, and pyrethrum, an insecticide.

▼ POLITICAL SYSTEM ▼

The Agikuyu did not traditionally have a central political system. They organized themselves around the clan system (which no longer operates). In the myth of origin, Gikuyu and Mumbi had ten daughters: Wanjiku, Njeri, Wambui, Wanjiru, Nyambura, Wangeci, Wangui, Waithera, Wairimu, and Wamuyu. The clans took their names from these daughters. The Agikuyu refer to their clans as being "nine and a fill," or "eleven minus one," not ten, because they fear that counting a living thing will bring it bad luck. All members of a clan were supposed to be distantly related to the daughter it was named after, and all the clans were related to Gikuyu, founder of the people.

Traditionally, the clan had rights to the land on which it lived. The clan kept contact with absent members through a group of leaders called Njama ya muhiriga. Law and order was in the hands of councils called Njama ya Kiama. Their main responsibilities were defending the community, punishing wrongdoers, settling land disputes and other problems, and advising young warriors.

The *kiama kia athamaki* or council of elders were responsible for hearing major disputes and pronouncing and enforcing judgments.

Among the Agikuyu, no one became a leader by birth or wealth alone. Leadership was earned by industriousness, intelligence, and the ability to compete. The leaders were expected to be hospitable, industrious, wise, brave, and

A Gikuyu chief dressed in the traditional clothes of his office.

intelligent, to command respect, to have clear visions about the community, and to be peace-makers.

Women were not included in mainstream politics and decision-making positions, although of course women can have all of the above qualities. They never participated in the council of elders, warrior councils, or Njama ya Kiama.

▼ HISTORY ▼

The name Gikuyu may have come from the word *mukuyu*, a kind of fig tree. The Gikuyu have therefore been called, "The people of the fig tree."

The Agikuyu use oral traditions as their main source of passing on history. Oral traditions are myths and stories passed on by word of mouth to serve as history for peoples who do not have a writing system.

According to oral tradition, it was at Muku-ruwe wa Gathanga in Murang'a district that the Agikuyu arose, multiplied, and dispersed.

Murang'a district is said to have been originally the land of the Gumba and Dorobo peoples. The Agikuyu acquired the land by peaceful negotiations and exchange for honey and animals. The Gikuyu adopted some of the Dorobos and intermarried with the Gumba. This encounter must have occurred before the 17th century.

Another popular myth that explains the origin of the Gikuyu concerns a man who had four sons. He called them to his deathbed to give them his possessions: a herding staff, a quiver of arrows with a bow, a stabbing spear, and a digging stick. The son who received the herding stick became the leader of the Maasai. The son with the arrows founded the Kamba people. The stabbing spear was the symbol for the Athi

group. Finally, the son who got the digging stick
became the first Gikuyu. The Gikuyu traditionally used digging sticks for farming.

An important aspect of Gikuyu life is initiation. At each generation, the boys who are of the
right age are initiated into manhood and receive
a group name. Each generation of Agikuyu is
known by its initiation name.

The study of *mbari* (genealogies) shows that
the Manduti and Cuma generations (from the
mid-17th to early 18th century) are remembered
for their raiding and hunting. The Mathathi and
Ndemi generations were a time of expansion,
when many Agikuyu migrated to different parts
of Kenya.

Some oral traditions say that the Gikuyu are
descendants of the Baci (Ethiopians); some
claim that they come from a Rendille man from
Meru who settled at Gathanga. Others trace
them to the Gumba or the Meru.

The myth of Mukurue wa Gathanga, or the
daughters of Gikuyu, acted as a symbol of unity.
From it emerged the idea of a single people
called the Agikuyu. The myth also legitimized
Gikuyu claims to land, because Ngai himself
gives the land to his people.

Sometime in the 19th century the Barabiu,
the Galla, and the Somali launched a major at-
tack in the Kenya highlands. Some Agikuyu
were driven back. The Barabiu were defeated

The Mukuyu, or figtree, is where Gikuyu, according to Agikuyu myth, built his first hut. It is considered a sacred place.

only after the allied forces of the Maasai, Athi, and Gikuyu attacked. That Agikuyu generation came to be known as the Iregi ("revolters"), to commemorate the defeat of the Barabiu.

In the 19th century the Maasai often intermarried with the Agikuyu. Thus a large percentage of people in Mathira and Tetu have some Maasai blood.

Between the Cuma and Ciira generations (late 17th to early 18th century) occurred a large expansion westward toward Nyandarua. The Agikuyu encountered Athi people, who offered little resistance. Reaching the Nyandarua

17

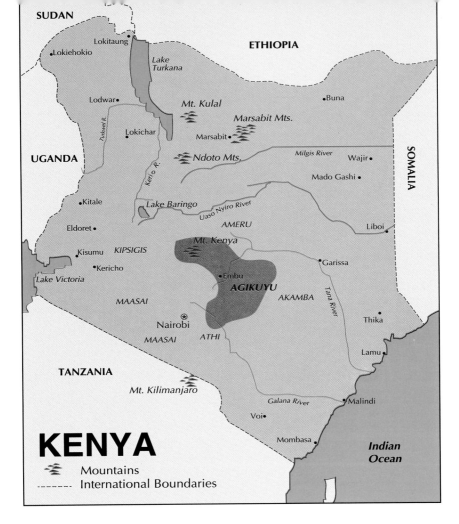

KENYA

≋ Mountains
------- International Boundaries

hills in the mid-19th century, they advanced southward to Muruka and Gatanga, where Maasai opposition began to worry them. In about a century, the Agikuyu had inhabited the area between the south Chania and Nairobi rivers. By 1890 pioneers had gone beyond the Nairobi River.

The Agikuyu came into close contact with many of their neighbors, especially the Maasai, the Akamba, and the Athi. Because the Maasai were mostly pastoral people, and the Agikuyu were mainly agricultural, these two groups had a

An Agikuyu coin featuring the first African president of Kenya, Jomo Kenyatta.

lot to offer each other. The Maasai depended on the Agikuyu for some grains and foodstuffs, while the Agikuyu traded for meat, hides, and other animal products. Becoming neighbors of the Maasai led to considerable borrowing. They adopted the concept of Ngai (God), as well as certain military tactics and initiation practices. The Athi were elephant hunters, and the Agikuyu traded with them for elephant meat and ivory. The Akamba were the best long-distance traders and for several generations had a working relationship with the Agikuyu, who were on their trade route from the Swahili coast.

The history of the Agikuyu was radically altered by events of the last quarter of the 19th century, which ended in colonization by the British. The Gikuyu attitude toward newcomers was influenced by the early behavior of Swahili caravans. They are traditionally hospitable people. However, the missionaries, settlers, and other representatives of Western imperialism were to betray this hospitality and trust.▲

chapter

2
TRADITIONAL LIFE

IN AGIKUYU SOCIETY, THE GROUP IS MORE important than the individual. A person might own land, but only as a representative of his family. In turn, a family's land or cattle were really held on behalf of the clan, and the possessions of a clan were owned by the entire community.

A group was made up of men and their wives and children. A woman would leave her own clan to join her husband's when she got married. When her sons got married, they would bring their new wives into the clan, but her daughters would join the clans of their husbands.

▼ AGE–SETS AND GENERATIONS ▼

Agikuyu think of their history in age-sets and generations. Each time an initiation ceremony

Membership in "generations" can be passed only from grandfathers to first-born grandsons.

takes place, the boys and girls who have passed through it are given a group name. This is their age-set name, and it links them for life.

"Generations" are more exlusive groups. The first group to be called a generation were the pioneers who found and cleared the land where the Agikuyu settled near Mt. Kenya. This group is now considered to be the heroic ancestors of the people. They are believed by some to have started the clan system. Only men can join new generations, and membership can be passed only from grandfathers to first-born grandsons who trace their lineage to members of the pioneer generation.

The Agikuyu traditionally believed in only one god. For them, Ngai is the creator of all creators, the divine father, the owner of brightness and mysteries. Gikuyu society believed in life after death. They believed that there was communication between the living, the dead, and generations yet unborn. This gave the community a deep sense of history.

Certain trees were thought to have supernatural qualities. The elders made sacrifices under these trees at ceremonies. The main sacrificial trees were the *mugumo* and the *mukuyu*; the *mukuyu* is the fig tree said to have given its name to the Agikuyu. Both trees were huge and rare. They were believed to have been planted by Ngai's own hands. They had no thorns and contained no poisonous substances. They were seen as trees of peace and reconciliation.

The Agikuyu had a ritual for every important event in the life cycle. When a baby boy was born, the people cried out five times to welcome it, and it was kept inside for four days. Four shouts were made for a baby girl, and she was kept indoors for three days. This difference in the treatment of boys and girls would continue for the rest of their lives. Rituals and customs would determine what a boy and a girl would become in the community.

▼ INITIATION ▼

Perhaps the major ritual in the life of a boy or girl was initiation. The boys were prepared at the age of puberty. They learned dances that symbolized their readiness to leave boyhood and become adults, responsible men in the community. Solemn dances, prayers, sacrifices, blessings, and lessons took place. After a long period of studying the customs of their people, the group of young men were initiated into manhood and given a generation name.

Girls were also initiated, but their adult lives were much different from those of men. Girl initiates were trained to forget their childish ways and to become good wives and mothers.

GIKUYU PRAYERS

The Agikuyu usually prayed facing Mt. Kenya, where Ngai was believed to live. They prayed before anything of importance was to be done. They were always sure to thank Ngai for all the goods things he had already done before they asked for any more favors.

Oh my father, great Elder
I do not have the words to thank you
But with your great wisdom
I am sure of your advice.

How I treasure your glorious gifts
Oh my father when I see how great you are
I am so full of awe that I cannot speak.
Oh great father
Ruler of all things on earth and in heaven,
I am your warrior,
Ready to do whatever you wish.

▼ MARRIAGE ▼

The ritual of marriage started with a long process of elaborate rituals and negotiations before the final marriage ceremony. A man had to receive permission to marry the woman he chose. Then a bridewealth was agreed upon, a quantity of livestock or goods that the man had to pay to his bride's father.

A recently married couple in their wedding ornaments. The bride wears a necklace of shells, which are considered sacred.

For women, marriage was a mixed blessing. It introduced them to a life in which they would become mothers and therefore win the respect of the community. But it also restricted them from free association with others and required obedience. They therefore used to sing *kiriro* (crying songs) during the first eight days of marriage, when they had to remain indoors.

For the man, marriage meant an addition to the family. Agikuyu men practiced polygamy, which means that they could have more than one wife at a time. A man who got married

A traditional Gikuyu wedding ceremony.

KIRIRO

A "crying song" sung by women who have just been married. The *kiriro* is sung during the first eight days of marriage, when the bride is not allowed to leave her husband's house. When she says she "dies alone" in the song, she means she is lonely and misses her freedom.

Oh dear
You of Gicui Village
You came to greet Waceera
She came here. She has drowned in the river
When the river dries up Waceera also dries up

I do not remember anything when you, our children,
    come in and go.
Waceera, did you leave that boy and Njeri well?
And now, I the lone child
You singer, when you reach aceera clan,
Greet Kigotho my father for me.
I know he did not come.
Ngewa, I have gone.
You greet Njeri.
Me, I died alone.
You know I will not
Be able to move freely.

I died alone.
Me, the lone child of Wangari.
You know I am no more able to move freely
Kigotho, my father,
May God be with you.

Storytelling was considered an important means of teaching.

showed that he was ready to be a responsible Agikuyu and command respect in the community.

▼ TRADITIONAL EDUCATION ▼

From the day a child was born, he or she was taught the ways and expectations of the community. A mother would sing lullabies:

Oh, keep quiet, my baby

Oh, Oh

Let those who were unhappy when you were
  born vanish.

Oh, keep quiet, my baby

Your mother will come and bring you ripe
  bananas.

Oh, keep quiet, your mother loves you more
  than anything else.

As the child was rocked to sleep, it also began to learn the rhythms of Agikuyu songs.

Children played many singing games, some

The Fourteen Falls are considered mysterious and sacred by Gikuyu elders.

simple, others very sophisticated. Through these games they learned the rules of the community.

Storytelling was also an important means of teaching. Every evening the children were told stories by their mothers, grandmothers, or aunts. The stories promoted virtues such as hospitality, hard work, bravery, perseverance, honesty, diligence, and tolerance. They discouraged cowardice, greed, laziness, and hasty decisions.

Children also learned by participation and observation. There was a clear gender division of labor. Girls accompanied the mothers to the fields and also helped in the domestic chores. They learned to weed, care for children, prepare food, and do other domestic chores. The boys, on the other hand, stayed with the fathers. They

GIKUYU PROVERBS

Indo ni kurimithanio. *Riches are found in cultivating together.* (There is great reward from working with others.)

Mwana ndetagia ithe nyama. *The son need not ask his father for a piece of meat.* (A parent should automatically give his child only the best.)

Rumwe rutiuranagwo, no kurikana rurikanaga. *The clan does not break, although its members separate.* (No matter where the clan members go, they are still part of the whole.)

Thiriti yagia kihehu no ithire. *Friendship finishes if there are whispers.* (Don't gossip!)

Muciri umwe ndagambaga. *One man alone in a council can say nothing.* (It takes several heads to make a big decision.)

Mubatari ndaconokaga. *A person in need is not ashamed.* (It's all right to ask for help.)

Igwa njithi itiri njohi. *Young sugarcane gives no beer.* (Be patient and wait until the time is right.)

Cionje ikumi irugitwo ni umwe uri na hinya. *Ten helpless people were surpassed by a single strong one.*

learned to watch animals, graze them, recognize animals by name and color, use a digging stick, make medicinal herbs, and roast yams and sweet potatoes. They learned their family lineage and the laws and customs of the community. Certain boys might also learn a special trade, such as blacksmith, diviner, or herbalist.▲

chapter

3

THE STRUGGLE FOR INDEPENDENCE

THE AGIKUYU LIVED A RELATIVELY PEACEFUL and simple life. Their main struggle was for survival, self-defense, creative living, and teaching their children to live a harmonious life. This existence ended when Great Britain invaded Africa and made it an imperial colony at the end of the 19th century. What resulted was a struggle for traditional lands and human rights, ending in the independence of Kenya from Britain in 1963.

Because the Agikuyu had some of the most fertile land in the region, they had one of the worst struggles with the colonists. The British sold the productive land to European settlers to raise cash crops that would bring in a good profit. The Gikuyu people were relegated to reservations that the British set up in arid areas poor for farming or grazing. Some Agikuyu

Not long ago, these tea plantations were dense forests.

families became squatters on white settlers' land; that is, they provided labor for the Europeans in exchange for being allowed to farm a little of the land.

By the early 20th century, the British were forcing the Agikuyu to work on communal projects, such as terracing the mountainside for farming and building a railroad. It was hard, unpaid labor. In addition, the colonial troops stole livestock, burned houses, raped women, and jailed men and women who resisted this brutality.

It is no wonder, then, that a resistance movement was born. Many men and women struggled against social, cultural, economic, and political oppression.

The Agikuyu had been hostile to all invaders from as early as 1870. At that time, the Imperial

British East Africa Company was trading in the area before Kenya had been colonized. The Company forced the Gikuyu men to become their porters through the difficult terrain.

In 1895 Kenya became a British colony. As the situation grew worse for the Agikuyu, many forms of rebellion took place throughout the country. The Agikuyu women refused to supply grain to traders, and their leader, Waiyaki Wa Hinga, was killed. Between 1902 and 1906 many expeditions were sent to Gikuyu land to force the people into submission. The people resisted, and many of them were killed by the British.

Settlers were encouraged to arrive, and more Africans were driven from their ancestral homes. More forced labor was necessary. The British also began to charge taxes, so the Africans had to find some way to earn money without having their land to produce income.

To earn money for taxes, thousands of people joined the migrating labor force. These were usually young men of the warrior age grade. They might go to harvest a certain crop in season, or to work on a railroad that the British were building through Kenya. Many people went to the cities, especially Nairobi, to find work.

The Agikuyu culture began to change, and oral tradition began to include songs of rebellion. In 1929, for instance, in the fight against

cultural oppression, the Agikuyu sang a famous
song called "Muthirigu":

> This land is ours
> This land is ours
> It was left for us by Iregi (those who resisted).
> The DC is a white man
> The priest is a white man
> You black man who
> supports the white man
> What tribe are you?
> I shall never leave my culture
> I shall never allow anybody to destroy it
> I, of the Agikuyu tribe,
> I am a Mugikuyu forever.
> This land is ours
> This land is ours
> It was left to us by Iregi
> We shall never let it go.

Many Agikuyu had been converted to
Christianity by the missionaries. However, the
Agikuyu could not continue to trust a church
that was accepted by a government that was so
cruel to them, and many broke away. Some
started independent churches.

The Agikuyu also began forming political
parties, such as the KCA (Kikuyu Central
Association). They often worked underground.
They planned to send some of their leaders to

A Gikuyu warrior.

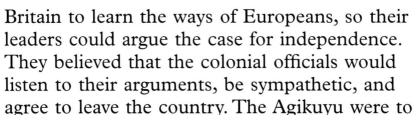

Britain to learn the ways of Europeans, so their leaders could argue the case for independence. They believed that the colonial officials would listen to their arguments, be sympathetic, and agree to leave the country. The Agikuyu were to learn that they were wrong. It was not a question of morality to the British.

In the meantime, heavy oppression continued. Many people were uprooted from Central Province and sent to the Rift Valley, where they lived in extreme suffering. They were beaten, isolated from other tribes, jailed, detained, and robbed of their property. Settlers forced the Africans to sell them even their goats and cows at the price the settlers chose. Child labor was also introduced in this period.

The people could not take it any longer. They organized themselves for armed struggle in a movement called Mau Mau. The Agikuyu took oaths to fight for the land and total freedom. The young men and women went to the forests and attacked the British government from every side. The struggle started in 1952. The people sang songs about the leaders of the fight for freedom. About Jomo Kenyatta they sang:

Kenyatta was arrested in October
He was guarded with guns
The white soldiers were shouting
"Let him be arrested and killed."

Let him be killed so that he stops working
   for Mau Mau
He was taken to Kapenguria
He was guarded with guns

The settlers also decided to arrest Odede
"Let us arrest him and jail him."
So that he stops supporting Mau Mau.

▼ WOMEN'S ROLE IN THE STRUGGLE ▼

Women had a great effect on the independence movement. They organized and spoke out courageously against injustice.

The Gikuyu women in 1947 protested against forced labor, especially public terracing activities. Women, who formed more than 50 percent of the labor force, laid down their tools against all administrative threats. They claimed that forced labor kept them away from their land and domestic work. As a result, the entire terracing project was stopped.

In 1930 Gikuyu women raised the money to build the Kiriri, a boarding school for girls. The women working on the project met violent resistance from the colonial government, who took over the building in 1952 and used it as a "death row" for people they intended to hang.

Women formed the backbone of the nationalist movement and later parties. In 1922 when the leader of the Young Kikuyu Association,

These Gikuyu elders were forced to renounce their support for the Mau Mau movement for fear of eviction from their homeland within the British-occupied areas.

Harry Thuku, was arrested, women took the initiative to demand his release, even by force. The story of Mary Nyanjiru is well known in Kenya. When Harry Thuku was held outside the Norfolk Hotel, Nyanjiru challenged the men to demand his release or take off their trousers and give them to the women. She was shot on the spot, and with her died many other patriots.

The Gikuyu rural women were the source of

The British greatly feared the Mau Mau movement. They even went so far as to evict from Nairobi all people suspected of being involved in it. Many Gikuyu people were forced to leave their homeland.

survival for many freedom fighters. Because they were on the run most of the time, they depended on food supplied by the village women.

The women also provided shelter to freedom fighters when their lives were in danger. Women also acted as couriers. Under the very eyes of security forces and homeguards, Gikuyu women smuggled guns, clothing, medicine, and other vital provisions to the freedom fighters.

Harry Thuku, right, was the leader of the Young Kikuyu Association in 1922.

In urban centers women spied on security forces and colonial administrators. They obtained information on their plans, operations, and movements, which they in turn communicated to the freedom fighters.

The Gikuyu women contributed to the Mau Mau freedom struggle because they believed in it. In their heroic efforts, they were raped, beaten, murdered, jailed, detained, and harassed. Gikuyu women's role in this struggle must be appreciated.▲

chapter

4

KENYA AFTER INDEPENDENCE

KENYA WON ITS INDEPENDENCE IN 1963. ITS first President was Jomo Kenyatta. Many people expected their lives to change drastically, particularly the Agikuyu, who had undergone great suffering for many years. However, this was not the case. Many former freedom fighters became disillusioned because they had no hope of getting back the land they had fought for. Field Marshal Muthone, an important leader in the Mau Mau movement, wondered why the freedom fighters were forgotten. She spoke out when she saw that many people who did nothing dangerous in the rebellion still ended up with all the power and money. They had the path cleared for them, "And they don't look back to see who took the risk."

Although many former freedom fighters felt disappointment, the spirit of the Harambee

Jomo Kenyatta was the first President of Kenya.

movement took root in the Agikuyu people.
Harambee is a Swahili word meaning "Let's work
together." Many started organizing to build
schools, hospitals, and health centers and to
engage in cash economy to support themselves.
The women's movement swept across the country. They collected money, bought land, and
worked on it.

The Kenyatta regime wanted those who had struggled to forgive the past and start afresh. They discouraged research on Mau Mau because such information would show that the current leadership did not reflect the spirit of the struggle. The general population resented those who did not participate in the struggle for freedom.

Leadership opposing the Kenyatta regime began to emerge, headed by Ngugi wa Thiong'o and Tom Mboya, among others. Ngugi wa Thiong'o was detained in 1978 after he wrote and produced a play, *Ngahika Ndeenda,* depicting the betrayal of those who had fought for independence. President Daniel arap Moi came to power in 1978.

The struggle against all forms of oppression was continued by prominent leaders who saw themselves as spokesmen for the nation of Kenya, not a particular people. They have a national vision; they champion the cause of justice for all Kenyans.

In post-independent Kenya, many newpapers and magazines have emerged through which the people's voice has been heard. Theater and popular music have been at the center of championing the struggle.

▼ URBANIZATION ▼

The Agikuyu live next to the capital city, Nairobi, in towns that have grown very rapidly.

Their lifestyle has been greatly affected by these urban centers. At first, people came to cities because there was no other way to earn money needed for taxes. Many people work as professionals or in factories and institutions. Thus cash or food-crop farming has been left to women. Children used to help with the farming, but the majority of children, both boys and girls, are in school.

Urbanization, Western education, Christianity, and interaction with many other foreign and local cultures have contributed to the end of tribal organization among the Agikuyu. Some of these changes are positive, others negative. The easy interaction between the rural and urban communities because of good communications has been a factor. Water and electricity have brought changes too.

Supporters of the tribal system maintain that what used to hold the people together is now gone. Extended families no longer stay together. Polygamy is little practiced. Many rituals and practices designed to fit the individual into a specific status in society have died out. This may be contributing to family and community problems. Many Gikuyu younger than thirty years can no longer tell you what clan they belong to. These might appear to be negative results of urbanization, Christianity, and other forces. It should be emphasized, however, that the death of tribal organizations has given rise to the birth of a nation. Many Gikuyu people see themselves as Gikuyu, but not as people of a specific clan. Their history in this century and their struggle for independence have created in them a spirit of nationalism. Even now they have difficulty thinking regionally.

▼ CHANGES IN CULTURE ▼

Culture among the Agikuyu continues to change. Certain rites and customs in initiation for girls, for example, are no longer seen as having value. Many Agikuyu send their sons to hospitals for circumcision because they believe it is medically safer. But the education process that accompanied the rites—which trained men to be brave and responsible and women to be good, submissive wives—is gone too.

Modern theater indicates that the culture of the Agikuyu is moving very fast. The famous Kamirithu Community Theater staged the play *Ngahika Ndeenda* ("I Will Marry When I Want") by Ngugi wa Thiong'o. That brought the detention of Ngugi wa Thiong'o by the Kenyatta regime. Since then, Gikuyu theater has been very active.

The artists have not only produced their plays in the National Theater and in hotels in Nairobi, but have staged European plays performed in the Gikuyu language. In a multiethnic,

The headpieces worn by the dancers are mantles from guereza monkeys.

multiracial society like that of Nairobi, this is an interesting move.

The other genre that expresses the current cultural changes is popular music. These artists have condemned the death of tribal culture, exploitation and oppression in all forms, and the marginalization of the Agikuyu by the Moi regime. Songs comment on the relationship between village and urban lives, and immoral life in society.

The leading popular singer is Joseph Kamaru, whose mastery of Gikuyu language and culture remains unchallenged. Kamaru is important for his use of the Gikuyu language and traditional

46

Many ceremonies and rituals, such as the dance that this young man is dressed for, no longer exist.

Some Gikuyu traditions have now become tourist attractions. Here, a healer performs one of his rituals for the benefit of tourists. The *mwano*, or divining gourd, on the right is used by the healer in his performance.

melodies. He is a social critic through his songs, many of which have been banned. His most famous song commemorates the death of the political leader J.M. Kariuki.

▼ WOMEN AND THE CHANGING CULTURE ▼

Gikuyu women and the women's movement have created an irreversible change. The movement as groups bought large pieces of land. The Nyakinyua movement saw to it that women had

It is the daughters of the Gikuyu women who will benefit from the ever-present struggle for autonomy.

control of resources such as land. Traditionally, women could not own land and did not inherit it. They could not own livestock. The women's movement has broken this tradition. For them and other Gikuyu women, the struggle for autonomy cannot be reversed. Gikuyu women such as Wangari Maathai, Eddah Gachukia, Martha Karua, and many more have become important leaders in their own right.▲

chapter

5

IMPORTANT AGIKUYU LEADERS

WAIYAKI WA HINGA. THE EUROPEAN ASKED FOR a little space and then demanded the whole country. Waiyaki wa Hinga met Captain Lugard, the flag bearer of the British East African Company, in 1890. Lugard was preparing the way for British imperialism in Kenya and Uganda. Waiyaki's struggle against the European's seizure of land and torture of the Agikuyu people led to one of the bloodiest encounters between Europeans and African nationalists. The Europeans ignored and undermined the goodwill treaty that Lugard had signed with Waiyaki. The British went around the country demanding food, goats, sheep, firewood, and women. In 1891 Agikuyu warriors overran the British fortress, and the British fought back with a vengeance. Waiyaki's resistance led to his death on August 17, 1892. Thanks to his efforts, the struggle for freedom was born.

50

Ngugi wa Thiong'o is the author of *The Trial of Dedan Kimathi*, a play about the influential leader of the Mau Mau movement.

Dedan Kimathi. Dedan Kimathi is the most famous Mau Mau general in Kenya. Plays have been written about him, including *The Trial of Dedan Kimathi* by Ngugi wa Thiong'o and *Micere Mugo and Dedan Kimathi* by Watene. Many myths and legends also surround him. Some myths say he could crawl for thirty miles, or even change himself into a white man.

Dedan Kimathi was born in 1920 in Nyeri district. He had a British education, and was very good at English and poetry. In 1941 he gave up his job as a primary school teacher to become an activist with the Kenya African Union. He was enthusiastic about the struggle for independence, and he became a secretary to the party.

He traveled around collecting money and spreading word of the cause. He also administered the oaths that were intended to commit people to the struggle. By 1952, Kimathi was known as the leader of Mau Mau. This placed him in command of all the armies in the forest. The Kenya Land Freedom Army entered the Nyandarua forests to begin the struggle against British rule. They established many guerrilla camps. Between 1953 and 1956 the British wrote several letters to Kimathi, calling for peace negotiations. He demanded the withdrawal of British forces before any peace talks. He published several newspaper articles appealing to the Kenyan masses to rally around the struggle.

The British brought reinforcements from home because of the Mau Mau refusal to give in. In 1957 Kimathi was arrested and hanged. But the struggle he had led continued.

Field Marshal Muthone was a warrior of great repute who worked closely with Field Marshal Kimathi and General Mathenge. She had been married for only one week when she and her husband joined the Mau Mau fighters in the forest. She was in the forest for 12 years,

THE GIKUYU MYTH OF WAGACIAIRI AND THE IRIMU

A blacksmith traveled to his smithy to work for several days. His wife Wagaciairi stayed at home. She was pregnant, and soon gave birth to her baby. An irimu (ogre) came to her with a bundle of firewood in his arms. "Wagaciairi!" he shouted, "may you fall with the same loud noise as this load makes when it falls." With this curse, he dropped the wood. "And you, too!" called the frightened Wagaciairi.

The next day the irimu came back and made the same curse. Then he prepared some food and offered it to Wagaciairi. He taunted her, "Wagaciairi, take this little food. If you don't want it, I shall eat it." And without waiting for her to reply, the irimu ate the food himself.

This went on for several days, and Wagaciairi was getting very thin. Then she noticed a dove in the doorway. She bribed the dove with castor beans to fly to the blacksmith and sing to him about what was happening.

The dove flew to the smith, and sang its song:

Blacksmith who smiths	*muturi uugutura-i*
cangarara-ica	*cangarara-ica*
Work quickly	*turatura narua-i*
cangarara-ica	*cangarara-ica*
Your wife has given birth	*muka-guo aanaciara-i*
cangarara-ica	*cangarara-ica*
With the ogre as midwife	*aaciarithio ni irimu-i*
cangarara-ica	*cangarara-ica*
"Wagaciairi, take this little food	*"Wagaciairi nduke tuhiuhio-i"*
cangarara-ica	*cangarara-ica*
If you don't want it I shall eat it."	*"na warega ngaaria-i."*

Every day for three days the dove sang this song at the smithy. At last the workers listened to it. "I left my wife pregnant," said her husband. "I must go to her!"

That day the smith returned to his wife. She hid him behind the house and they waited for the irimu. The irimu came and dropped his daily bundle of firewood, saying "Wagaciairi, may you fall with the same loud noise as this load makes when it falls." The woman was not frightened, and the irimu got suspicious. "Why are you acting as if the blacksmith had come home?" "Stop laughing at me. He'll come," warned Wagaciairi. With that her husband grabbed his spear and killed the irimu. The irimu's last words were,

I said that the blacksmith had come!	*Noo njugire, noo njugire mari uturi ni mookiite!*

and came out only in 1963, when Kenya won its independence.

Jomo Kenyatta was born in 1897 of peasant parents in Kiambu district. He went to a mission school, and by 1918 he was working in Nairobi.

In 1924 he became interested in politics, and joined the Kikuyu Central Association (KCA). There he met James Beautah, Joseph Kan'ethe, and other patriots who were questioning the legitimacy of the Europeans in Kenya. Kenyatta helped to draft letters and responses to the colonial government. By 1928 he was a well-known figure in the KCA. He launched the first newspaper written in the Gikuyu language, *Muigwithania,* which became the voice of the Agikuyu.

In 1929 Kenyatta was sent to England to represent the KCA's grievances to the British commission. In 1932 he was sent for military training in Moscow. Returning to Kenya in 1938, he helped start independent schools. At this time he wrote his famous books *Facing Mt. Kenya* and *My People the Kikuyu.*

Kenyatta was arrested by the British in 1952 and detained for seven years. They feared he had been involved in the Mau Mau movement. When Kenyatta was released, he became the President of the Kenya African National Union (KANU). In 1963 he was elected the first President of Kenya. He died in 1978.

Harry Thuku, a pioneer of African nationalism in Kenya, was born in 1885 in a poor family. In 1914 he joined the British East African
Newspaper in Nairobi to learn printing. In 1921
Thuku became president of the Young Kikuyu
Association, which soon became the East
African Association (EAA). It was the first company organized against colonial measures. The
EAA sent a petition to the colonial secretary
in London, and held meetings to protest the
government.

Harry Thuku was arrested in March 1922 for
his participation in the EAA. During a demon-
stration in Nairobi against the arrest, British
troops fired and killed twenty people. Thuku was
deported to Mombasa and sent to the Kismayu
Islands to cut him off from his political connec-
tions. Thuku spent nine years in detention.
When he returned to Kenya in 1930 he continued to work toward the political freedom of
his people.

Wangari Maathai is a scientist and professor
in Kenya. She was the chairperson of the
National Council of Women of Kenya (NCWK)
and extremely vocal on women's issues and
nationalism. She started a project called the
Green Belt Movement, and through it has
become a national leader in environmental
issues.

Wangari single-handedly struggled to bar the

Wangari Maathai began the Green Belt Movement and has become a national leader in environmental issues.

government from building a skyscraper at Uhuru Park because it was environmentally unsound. She lobbied even with the British government, arguing that they should not support the project because they would never have allowed it to be built in Britain. She won the battle.

Dr. Eddah Gachukia, a leader in the field of education, is currently executive director of the Forum for African Women Education Ministers and Vice Chancellors in Nairobi. Dr. Gachukia is also a Senior Lecturer at the

The Agíkuyu are proud of their history and are working hard to keep it alive.

Department of Literature of the University of Nairobi. She has championed the right of women and girls to have education that would empower them to participate in all levels of decision-making.

Dr. Gachukia has been a member of the Kenyan Parliament for ten years and is a founding member of the African Women Communication and Development Network.▲

CONCLUSION

The Agikuyu people have had a difficult century. In a way, they were one of the luckiest peoples in Kenya, because they had some of the finest land available. But because of that fact they became the obvious targets of the British colonial government. The Agikuyu situation became worst than most, and their numbers were larger. Because of this, and because of the courage of some remarkable people, the Agikuyu were leaders in the long, hard fight for Kenyan independence.

Not much of traditional Agikuyu culture is still practiced. The tribal system has fallen apart, and young men and women are getting an urban education and living in a modern way. However, the roots of the Agikuyu are strong. They are proud of their history, and their language and customs are being studied and recorded by people who are determined to keep that history alive.

Glossary

Baci Ethiopians; possibly ancestors of the Agikuyu.

clan Group of people within a tribe who believe they are descended from the same ancestor.

gicandi (1) Musical instrument made of a gourd with seeds inside; (2) poetry contest involving the *gicandi*.

Gikuyu (1) The Agikuyu. (2) In myth, the offspring of Ngai, and father of the Agikuyu people.

initiation Ceremony by which boys and girls pass from childhood into adulthood.

kiama kia athamaki The clan council of elders.

Kikuyu Another spelling of Gikuyu.

Kiriri Boarding school built by the women's movement to provide good education for girls.

kiriro "Crying song" sung by new brides to lament the end of their freedom.

Mau Mau Militant movement of freedom fighters struggling for independence from the British in Kenya.

mbari Genealogies (family trees) of the Agikuyu.

mugumo A sacred tree.

mukuyu Fig tree that perhaps gave its name to the Agikuyu people.

Mumbi In myth, the wife of Gikuyu, and mother of the Agikuyu people.

Ngai The Agikuyu god.

Njama ya kiama The clan council responsible for keeping in touch with clan members who have left the area.

Njama ya muhiriga The clan council responsible for law and order in the community.

polygamy Having more than one wife at a time.

squatters African people who lost their own land and had to live on the land of European settlers.

terracing Public-work project to cut terraces in mountainsides so that they could be used as farmland.

For Further Reading

Barra, G. *1000 Kikuyu Proverbs*. London: East African Literature Bureau and Macmillan, 1960.

Bendon, T.G., and Barlow, A. Ruffell. *English-Kikuyu Dictionary*. Oxford: Clarendon, 1975.

Kabira, Wanjiku Mukabi. *The Oral Artist*. Nairobi: Heinemann Educational Books, 1983.

Mockerie, Parmenas Githendu. *An African Speaks for His People*. New York: AMS Press, 1977.

Mugo, E.N. *Kikuyu People: A Brief Outline of Their Customs and Traditions*. Nairobi: Kenya Literature Bureau, 1982.

Muriuki, Godfrey. *A History of the Kikuyu, 1500–1900*. Nairobi: Oxford University Press, 1974.

Sangren, David P. *Christianity and the Kikuyu: Religious Divisions and Social Conflict*. New York: P. Lang, 1989.

Throup, David. *Economic and Social Origins of Mau Mau, 1945–1953*. London: J. Currie; Athens: Ohio University Press, 1987.

Waciuma, Charity. *Daughter of Mumbi*. Nairobi: East African Publishing, 1969.

Index

ABOUT THE AUTHOR

Wanjiku Mukabi Kabira received both a BA and an MA in literature and recently received her doctorate.

Dr. Kabira is the author or coauthor of seven books, including *Kenya Oral Narratives, Gikuyu Oral Literature,* and *Black Aesthetics,* and has five other publications forthcoming. She has also published numerous papers and several short stories.

Dr. Kabira is affiliated with several organizations. She is Chairperson of the Kenya Oral Literature Association, and Co-Chairperson of the Association of African Women in Research and Development. She has organized several workshops with these and other groups.

Dr. Kabira lives in Nairobi, Kenya, where she is a lecturer in the Department of Literature at the University of Nairobi.

Photo Credits: AP/Wide World (pp. 38, 39, 42); Nation Newspapers, Inc. (pp. 40, 51, 56); CFM, Nairobi all other photos
PHOTO RESEARCH: Vera Ahmadzadeh with Jennifer Croft
DESIGN: Kim Sonsky